Dried Flowers

AF624476

Bhagyashree Parchure

BookLeaf Publishing

Presentation by *BookLeaf Publishing*

Web: www.bookleafpub.com

E-mail: info@bookleafpub.com

ISBN: 978-93-5721-577-0

First edition 2023

DEDICATION

To mom for moulding me into the person I am today and Pops for his unconditional love.
To Binni for the words unspoken and Abhi for being nothing but supportive and encouraging.
To Snober ma'am for exposing me to the world of English literature.
And to you who have decided to stick with me all along.

CONTENTS

Incipient
/ɪnˈsɪpɪənt/ Beginning to happen or develop.

Chatoyant
/ʃəˈtɔɪənt/ (Of a gem, especially when cut en cabochon) showing a band of bright lustre caused by reflection from inclusions in the stone.

Panegyric
/ˌpanɪˈdʒɪrɪk/ A public speech or published text in praise of someone or something.

Penultimate
/pɪˈnʌltɪmət/ Last but one in a series of things; second last.

incipient

The seeds of your heart

Now, I am not the one
who would push your beliefs
or make you appreciate sorcery
or some inscriptions on a leaf.

But hear me out when I say.
There is this one thing I find very very interesting.

Imagine the big bang
The creation of this tiny earth
The mass of matter in our cosmos
has never risen or shattered.

Inch and inch of our body
belongs to something superior.

The breaths we take the puffs we let out
all have witnessed everything from dusk till dawn
From the big bang to
millions of people's whereabouts

but hear me out when I say
there is this one thing I find very very interesting

There are infinite scores of beauty
in everything you oh so profoundly hate.
Infinite answers

in all the unsettled debate
For sure we have long since stopped roaming,
our atoms uncompressed just floating

Now I am not the one
who would push your beliefs
but they have decided to make
your crooked existence their home in peace.

I won't need magic or written inscriptions to let you know
the seeds of your heart were planted fourteen billion years ago

People are not works of poetry.

You can get up early
write for endless hours
put your sweat and blood into it but know that:

People are not works of poetry.

Sure, you want to hold on to their memories
write small prose easy remedy
before you do tell me

will the poem have observations to what degree?

It's okay if you are shattered
a little rough, disfigured
You want to write so much that your memories alter

Will these poems also be about the defaulter?
Poems need arrangement
the way you button your dress
you will have to rethink all the arguments

People are more like monuments

You want to escape
you want to let go of all the bottled up
no longer wear the red cape

will all this be written... condensed into a single
metaphor?

It's completely okay to not know what you are doing
unlike poems, feelings don't really rhyme
the poem is immortal once completed take your time
no hurry

but remember People are not works of poetry.

All fallen leafs account for a beautiful scene

The leaves grew.
flowers dying as they fall,
they resemble shredded pages
from one of the most favorite books, you can recall

Each leaf, each flower
is a brown-black song a beautiful tale,
an unread, thoughtless chapter
dramatic novel, epic, fairytale

But consider a wildfire
Perhaps not in antiquity,
but the massive smoke continuously
burnt parchment in your proximity.

Take the fading colors
and dying beauty in your arms.
tell yourself its just fire
not the end of it all

soon it will be spring
soon the foliage will turn green
I know right now it's scary
but remember all fallen leafs account for a beautiful
scene

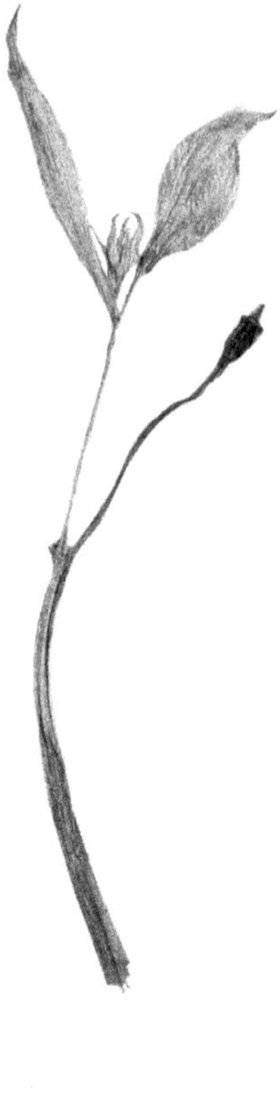

Let me introduce you to the art of drowning

Isn't it astonishing?
We. You and me
we exist?

Some of us try to end it
not knowing what it means or what it meant
Wait wait hold on, let me introduce you
to the art of drawing with pure intent

You lie down
let reality grip you by your throat
and suddenly you start to float

Your life might flash before your eyes
heck, you might also see how time flies by
the heart slows it's pounding
this is what I call the art of drowning

Compress compress decompress
the medics will try to drain your fluids
questioning your sanity and your real intents
Some of us try to end it
knowing its a criminal offense
but, Wait hold on let me introduce you
to the art of drawing with pure intent

Trust me it felt like a crime

Do you remember that odd evening
the moon fell from the sky?
And we dashed through the woods to find out why?

Giggling scrambling dogging the roots
we ran like kids
Twigs in heads and mud stuck on our boots

You were holding hands
swearing we would never let go
the falling moon was just a reason though

When we finally found it
when we actually saw it lying on the cold cold ground
everything started to compound

leaves stuck in our hair
cheeks redder than a rose to compare
out of breath we looked at each other

Was that all?
phrases to express stuck in our throats
a day that I can clearly recall

We took a walk back
not holding hands this time
trust me it felt like a crime

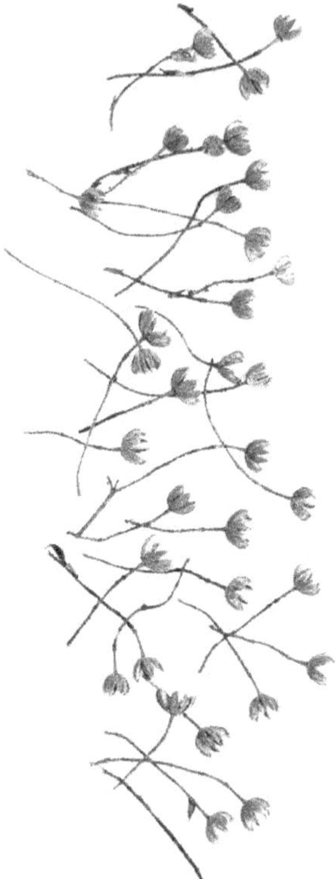

Your figure, your silhouette

Your rich red structures
represent the sun at its full glory,
all of your equations decorated with dried flowers,
a whole new story.

When it's dark,
And the clouds are roaring,
your limbs are thrashing,
your voice feels rehearsed and reality slowly detaching

That unusually well-kept hair
was slaughtered in the depths of night,
as the sun slept in our garden
a pure delight

Yes to twilight over the land
to the deep dark lake, half burnt cigarette
to your black hair scented with moonlight
Your figure, your silhouette

From the midnight free drafts,
conspiracy to sincerity,
sea supremacy
shades dominancy

The game of shadows was characterized
by the lovers of the unknown

love as dark, voracious, and brown
an image that no word can ever account

Your rich red structures
represent the sun at its full glory,
all of your equations decorated with dried flowers,
a whole new story.

Me a gold ribbon in the sky.

My fingers clenched on fluff,
against everything I had ever genuinely held on to.
I was attempting to keep my flesh and bones intact.
But there was something in that motion that I couldn't
call out to.

Was as much a piece of me
as I am of God.
And I'd realized I didn't have anything.
Because I already had it all,

Me a shattered gold ribbon in the sky.
As each and every star keeps falling.
All I could conjure of was this
mess of a poem an act of forestalling

When I revived,
the sky was a brilliant blue,
with no proof of it ever being shattered.
not knowing what was true

The cosmic eye blinked
beside the crashing breeze howling
Me a gold ribbon in the sky.
As each and every star keeps falling.

No meaning or a single human in sight

Some people only a sentence,
while others occupied long, long prose,
stretched out in rows and floors.

Thousands of inky footprints were left behind
but in fact, there was
no meaning or a single human in sight

Why write about characters you've met before?
Why dwindle on things that wash up the shore?
Why spend energy writing poetry or prose?

All the books in this heart lack notary
Will this pile of debris be worth a penny
some would just propose psychiatry

Ink running through the walls
manic passive each and every character
was more than just involved

Bookshelves getting overloaded
while the typewriter in the room half flooded
kept going type type ding

Collections of memories collecting dust.
Titles like "Who do I trust,"
but not a book worth a discuss

Thousands of inky footprints were left behind
but in fact, there was
no meaning or a single human in sight

Pull the green ribbon, I mean it.

I'm not sure what it means to exist,
about having these breaths.
All I do is keep puffing in and choking on
the idea that I am imperfect.

In every pair, with different variations
there exist the same conflict,
but at this point in time pull the green ribbon and oh I
mean it

I am up till the moon sets
trying to keep my green ribbon intact
holding my emotion and reasoning
in the same bed, head to body contact.

And trust me knowing you are treasured
and feeling you are loved are two different things
Like snow in the middle of spring

However, somewhere along the road,
it convinced me that I was more
more than what's occupying this body,
there was more than the green ribbon at my core

So will letting go of this green ribbon free me?
or I'll be getting plunged
into another unsolvable mystery?

makes love feels nothing more
than a charity
I really don't understand
this green state of insularity

I believe I am doing my best to love you,
holding the green ribbon
but given the choice pull the green ribbon and oh I
mean it

Rather than lying holding the ribbon intact
set me free,
let me go
let the body and head have no contact

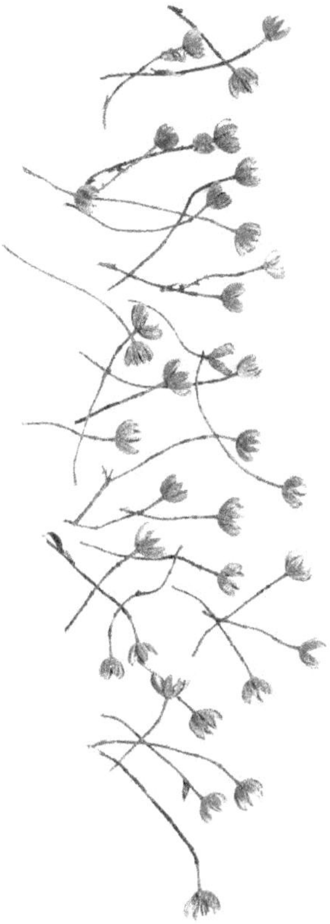

A broken heart is not covered under insurance

So rather than stepping out,
I was schooled to up the ante.
I've been the same since
managing resources even when they were scanty

This was a strategy
for keeping me secure.
I was trained to up the ante
before plunging too deep to ever come back to shore.

So rather than sharing secrets
I test a man thrice
I was instructed that respect must be earned.
everything has a price

So rather than giving it a go
I dabble my boots in assurances,
being quite cautious with my emotions.
A broken heart is not covered under insurance

But, rather than feeling fine
Everything seems like it's overflowing
your depths appear to be the safest place
and all the seeds you planned growing

So rather than keeping my secrets hidden.
as there isn't any time to up the ante;
I'm leaping in headlong swinging down the bay
with no sense of security handy

So please don't crush my faith
when I strike the sea.
I was instructed to up the ante
to all way up the ante

chatoyant

I don't blame people for being religious

comforting escape being suspicious
At times the cold weather makes me go numb too
making things foggy and covering what's true

But I think this dark cold season
will retain my soul
God has not been comforting
But I would love to explore what's unfolding

Oh there is a lot of misery
I don't even know how to express my thoughts
There is no style like realism

and things will not always be this way,
because no matter how long they last
seasons inevitably change
But its the religion that never strange

So even in the cold morning winds
Which are blazing in my mind
I am steady in my core
Its religion nothing more

In the dead of winter,
I will try to keep on living

no matter what was taken,
It's in my nature to keep on giving.

I don't blame people for being religious
A little bit of magic or being superstitious.

Greenlands

Come running through the forest
of these thoughts
and collapse
into my arms.

Run through the wilderness
of who and what did not want you
and realize there is freedom for you
to still want better things.

It is okay to dream better dreams.
Even if what you lost
seemed to be everything.
Because the truth is,

you were always made for more.
You were always made to carry on
through the worst of things,
gathering all the strength you would need

to be who you are today.
Even when you were hurt along the way.
Even when you felt like a prisoner
in your very own mind, by grace,

you survived
and you still have permission

to roam free.
Roam free into the clearing.

Catch your breath.
Fall.
Rest.
Begin again.

You are allowed to do that.
You are allowed to want more
than these current feelings
and out in the clearing,

A cyclone that leaves no trace

Even in the midst of the chaos
that has raged through my mind today,

I am okay I'll be fine

when the weight of it all becomes too much,
my soul remains steady with everything that I hold so much

It's true, since my childhood
and no amount of darkness could sway my winds

I have overcome so many obstacles.
even though I have slammed my face and have some regret

She was insignificant.
more than a broken thread,

I want to be reminded by grace
as the cyclone who leaves no trace

That’s all the tea in my cup

Yes, I have grown
Learned to deal with things all alone

I do have people all around me
But freeze or fight? I always flee

I am under construction
And I like it like that

I have a lot of mysteries
These also include my tiny victories

And that's all that
Expect me to skip small chat

I don't want people to know me
Not two present or to any other degree

That's how I was brought up
That's all the tea in my cup

well, I have grown
Learned to deal with things all alone

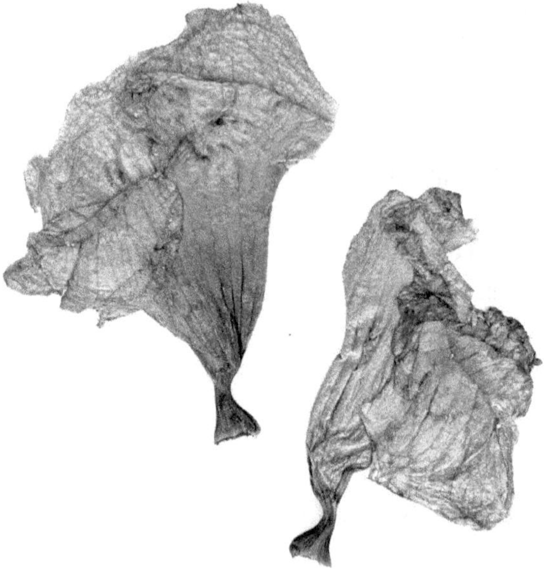

Getting lost

I want to get lost
on the highway of happiness
but I end up taking turns that leads me to regrets
and dunes of emotional debts

I want to find myself walking through memories,
not the ones that I'd been trying hard to forget,
but of my father throwing me in air
all the rollercoaster rides in that west town fairs

Sadness and misery always hidden in plain sight
growing out of cracks in the sidewalk, finding way up
the wall
With thorns grown so sharp that they promised,
To pierce my young heart if I should fall

These memories spread endlessly,
Until they were too far away to be seen,
so spread that that's all that could be seen
that's now my reality it has always been

There tucked beneath all the brambles,
Were memories I'd long since forgotten,
Pieces of proof that my lifetime,
Wasn't just made of things that were rotten,

These dried flowers had changing colors
From the moment that I had been born,
lost sight of the sunlight,
beautiful black and brown

And as I stumbled back onto the highway,
I knew there was much more to learn,
But in a world that is fearful of failing,
I was glad that I made a wrong turn.

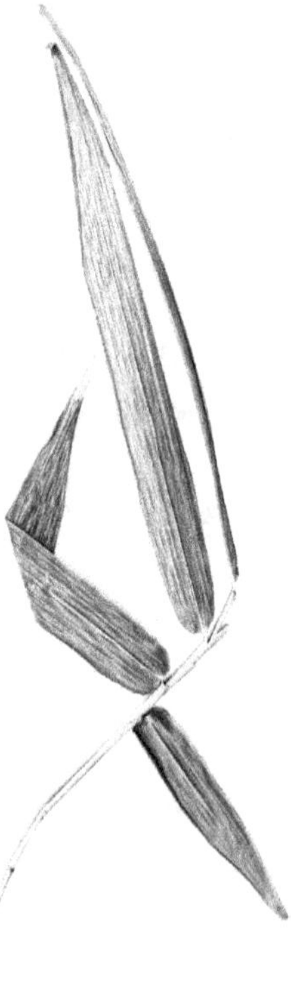

Empty and shallow

If you break open my lifeless body
You will find empty space cold and bloody

I was never like this
There is nothing wrong says my therapist

I feel like a dotted pale line
In a painting, post impressionist style

Tried drugs to numb the pain,
Naked empty but bound with a chain

You have come so far.

I would love to live each day
as if it's my first
As if I just took birth

Experiencing everything
as I open my eyes
breathe the nectar just to surfice

Take first steps and drop in my mother's arms
make new friends and hand around on the barn
marry the love of my life till death do us apart

I believe that is the secret of immortality
Living each day
Forgetting all rationality

Worrying about me when you are gone.

Love

They yell and scream that love is nothing more than a lesson in history
But you are here on your deathbed, worrying about me when you are gone
It's simple and very clear, I will just follow you along
When the peasants decide to over through you
I'll be standing still ready to get stoned to death too
I'm not going to cry for you.
I'm not going to condemn what you do.
I'm not going to cry for you
I am going to follow you in the next real walk on glass if I have to

Love

We are not just sculptures for Michelangelo to carve.
He can't undo the damage done by my enraged heart.
I'll wait on the frigid mountain tops of Paris.
or sunken below the shallow sea in Venice
I don't want to die alone.
but you are here on your deathbed worrying about me when you are gone

People can’t be your home

Did no one teach you?
People can't be your home
Even if it's the bestest that you have combed

People are like sea
Living in their own mystery
Look at sir Vincent van Gogh’s history

People are like sea
You give them all, down on one knee
Just to flee

People are like see
You can give then your heart
But remember the moon will always keep you apart

Let me teach you
People can't be your home
Even if it's the bestest you have combed

panegyric

Wish to be here

You miss your mum
when you have to close the door.
Love and pain when you must leave,
but—come back with our hearts on your sleeve;

Please tell me you weren't hungry that day.
Tell me that wasn't your initial attraction.
Seven seeds do not appear to be a convincing
cause to reject a mother's sensitive compassion.

I'd like to believe you had a choice;
that you heard more than my voice;
and that you stretched your palms to offer your heart
rather than meet my expectations carte.

Persuade me you want to be here;
this isn't a ruse to keep you so near.
You have chosen me.
You are crazy about me.

There's no need to justify your departure.
I'm not going to obstruct you or make it harder.
Simply state that you were not hungry on that specific day.
Simply tell me that I'm the reason you will stay.

Just wish to be here, and I will believe.

On the grounds you'll find me;

without crushing, splitting, or fading
just touch the willowing flowers
The days will be happier,
and my nights will be calmer,

We can call me by your name,
if I live in the grasslands, wet barks, or rain;
yet as the sun sets and fresh life emerges,
I will expire in the clay.

My face will be hurting,
my pulse may be elicited,
my lips will be closed,
and my hands will show bruises.

I'll live there,
and my grave will lament the names;
You will come along the sky and farm on my ashes,
growing lavender granges.

And when you walked along the grounds,
I reside; it would struggle and detain you.
As time passes and the earth revives,
under the dying stars.
I'm going to be one of those.
Present in raindrops to butterflies.

My voice will reverberate through the darkness.
And may you find me in every moment of my life.

When a ten dozen moons passed above me,
whether it's a bug or a bright light in the sky.
I'd see you smiling every time
I looked at you from my closed shrine.

6 ft under

The clouds sobbed.
Flooding the naive dirt, drop by drop

I watched the petals gently giving way as autumn leaves fell.
The scarlet of a kiss engraved on the neck, his presence casting a spell

Everything is greyscaled.
The sky, the land, everything on which his fingers trailed

He was racing about in the middle of the night.
A fragile being who, once gone, will never be back in sight

Never gazing at the falling leaf on the land of dream,
Never having heard the wind moan or the rain scream,

Never experiencing the loving fog,
Delicacy of a dew drop

The clouds sobbed.
Flooding the naive dirt, drop by drop

Solidarity

I never figured out why individuals craved solitary.
I had always been alone when I desired others in my company.

My entire life has seemed solitary, among a throng,
like seeing smiling tokens through a window for too long.

My memory fades. I need experiences to keep me sane.
To keep me snug when I'm alone something to revisit agin and again...

Have you ever sat alone while listening tranquilly?
It is deafening, vacant, and lifeless, as if you are summoning darkness

It made me reckless... A hyperreal nightmare.
But one thing is certain

Experiences don't require anyone.
And even if it did, you didn't force an abandoned building for assistance.

RAIN IN MY HEART

My soul is peaceful
as if it had slept from days of torture.

Meanwhile,
the skylight blackbirds are singing in the pouring rain.

Thunderstorms on the roof;
rain in my soul;
while experience slumber beneath the grey, windless sky,
bringing no illusions of any well-remembered day.

I wouldn't even have gorgeous skies,
shimmering hues,
or wind rustling, but days like these,
until my soul is healed from the absence of you.

I'm not going to see you.
Every wish to understand you in your current state has passed away.

I who have matured,
would not find the face I loved so drastically changed.

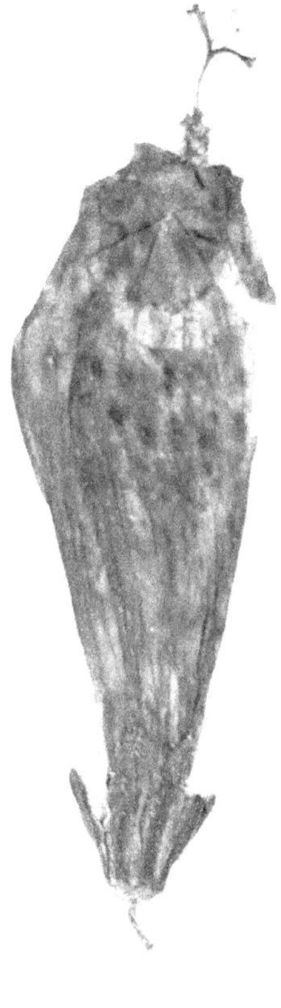

A Beltane Blessing

Let flowers always line your spirit,
and sunlight always leads the way.
Wish that you never regard
what others have to say.

If you stretch a sincere hand,
fate will rise to welcome you.
Let the kindness of unfamiliar people demonstrate
how most wonderful things happen by chance.

Let the best of accomplishments
be how often love you give.
wish you always be delighted
of the life you've quilled.

Let your family and loved ones
boost you up when you feel inadequate.
Let their existence in your spirit
always be its own advocate.

And if you come across
a proudly unveiled soul to appreciate,
let that courage teach you
to still exhibit your own.

Pain has a new name

The sorrow will linger lightly.
You'll try to gently sweep it as you go about your day,
but you'll quickly understand it intends to stay.

It hangs around in the background.
It pursues you everywhere.
Only when you believe that you have everything
figured out
You discover that there is no consolation to be sought.

So here's a technique I've picked up over the years:
Agony and I have been dear old friends.
And suffering is scared of love, since love ultimately
heals.

So, widen your vision a tiny bit.
Take a few deep breaths vigorously.
Search for the glimmer of beloved's warmth
that surrounds you throughout the day.

It's all around. A wish, a cheesy grin, a gesture
Seek affection in any situation.
And your discomfort will begin to diminish.

Simply begin modestly, why not do it now?
Think up something creative.

'When you focus on love, pain will flee,'
mark my words, you will see!

And as painfully and in pieces
you hack at the pain
you will realise
The pain now has a new name.

Tomorrow, a hypothesis.

However, life never appears.
The last gasp is hanging on our tail,
Nonetheless, we continue to choose not to flee.
And now we're in a new day.

Everything is flowing past our fingertips,
As we turn the other cheek,
Hours, weekends, years, and decades
are composed of the present ticks.

A series of transient events,
that we will never be able to record.
We look ahead
as if it's where we're destined to be.

However, life never appears.
The last gasp is hanging on our tail,
Nonetheless, we continue to choose not to flee.
And now we're in a new day.

Anxiously anticipating that same day,
When we can say we're content,
we spend so much time gazing
ahead that we could equally be blind.

Considering we really shouldn't see all the possessions
we've left behind until the very final moment,

I realize it's only a hypothesis, but I think I've figured out how,
The only route to peace is to appreciate what we have right now.

To just get up and disappear

I like to act as if I died
Begging divine to let me be back in my mother's sight.
Begging him to grant me a rebirth
I wish to relive my life on earth.

Yes, I want to die.
a lot more than this passing breath
but is surprising how much I would love
to start from the bottom and regrow my wealth

Every day, I would come to an end.
running through the forested valleys
Swimming in deep blue bays
getting lost in new familiar alleys

I'd appreciate being sentimental.
over the things I despise
attempt to do all thing
things I once desired to design

It's not that I've made a lot of mistakes.
No, I don't have anything I'd desire.
it's just this urge,
in my core innate
to just get up and disappear.
end what the diving creates

penultimate

We might not have the best relationship...

People generally guess,
I always look up to you.
Maybe even try and sparkle like you a second or two.

I'm just a blip, a dot of flame and once moisture.
On this wide, brash beach, a lovely oyster.
The future is bright; I will never reach it as this.

The rising hours are pale in colour.
Why don't we mix them up?
The morning light a blend of orange and pearl;

She is a beautiful young brat, resuscitating in the east,
creeping up the ladder, just to disintegrate in the west.
I a lousy role model at its best.

My soul bows in your wake,
euphoric at the glimpse of you: how devoted, how true!
I desire everything, everything, all of it; I despise the blue.

You, splendid and bright, bring dishonour to the Cosmic panorama.
You are the most important connection, towering over us all.
Why are you still powdering your dust and spring cleaning uncalled?

I am pastel pale.
I've been crushed by feet,
wanting you to crave the colour I'll never be.

and you? abundant me now that I am haze-free.

A slit on my skin

I have a certain slit
That is embroidered on my skin
It has all of the key moments, happy, sad, and grim

All the ones I believe to be my most significant
And when a pal mentions something that makes them
happy or feel insignificant,
I fit it bit by bit in my slit,

As a result,
I keep them for a long.
holding on tight and carrying it everywhere all along

And when I'm feeling depressed, like I was today,
I'll tug on one of the
stranded cotton strings
To relieve the despair

The slit is never completely empty.
however, occasionally overflow.
never in a way that overloads

And the love that flows out of
it is how the slit that I call my heart develops,
and perhaps the slit extends
If I embrace you extremely close.

I'll keep writing and writing

something you can read now and then
A story of how we could be,

in a universe where you are sacred and free

We'd go places close and far, strolling barangays
just the two of us and endless days

Our soles could transport us almost anywhere.

Our hands would remain bound.
Even if one of us was crowned

So when the moon begins to pale away

Just tell me what you want to write,
and I'll keep writing and writing

As if writing defines our destiny

I could write about us for the rest of the time.
If you let my imagination go wild.

I'd write us onto mountain peaks.
where we could play like kids

I'd write us into all the wonders yet to be seen,

I'd write us onto sea sides.
where we watch the sunset and tides

To begin with let me write YOU into existence

To lie with you

on a field of grass
to lie down and watch
the world pass us by

gently rubbing
palms and thigh
neither of us asks why

neither wishing for more
to have the full length
of your freezing body

down my own path
to find the power
of a buried tide

Desire penetrates
into our veins and goes
deep...deep.

Dissolving flesh and melting bone
To be honest,
I'm not sure.

alone
To notice your breasts
rising in response to my moan

To maintain your image
in my mind's eye
Neither wishing for more

Your bits

I'd like to take tiny bits of you
that I adore,
and press them like flowers.

I want to save them all, like shreds
from between the pages
of my favorite book.

Collect whatever you don't like
about yourself,
put them in my freezer.

To prove,
I am proud of you
and only because it's true.

I want to twirl you like a planet,
when we dance,
cherish every aspect of who you are.

Gliding my finger over your naked body,
till it stopped to find the bits of you.
Bits I never knew.

I'd want to wrap them,
in linen that you haven't revealed
even those bits that are heeled

I'd put them in an
old vintage box and
hide them away. carefully.

I keep it in the sock drawer
of my bedside table,
hit them with no labels

When you share,
let those bits of yourself go.
Just speak your mind let it flow.

You're putting your faith in me
in an individual who truly loves you
honey, I'll hold on to them in your absence

Can I ask for a refund on this soul?

I still belong to myself,
no matter how many times
I try to give myself away.

No matter how many slits and cuts,
thought of a knife to my guts.
Selling my soul to satan for some gluts.

I'll always be mine.
No matter how many times,
someone tries to take it away from me.

Letting go of the wheel,
sliding down a bus.
The body? Perish. Consciousness is still truss.

The soul, the body.
Two beliefs,
two cores
two fires,
one whole.
Two individuals,
two designers,
but still a singular structure.

I don't want to be in their
insane or sadly sane worlds,
and I don't want this body or this core

Can I ask for a refund on this soul?

Gaping unaccounted hole

There is a gaping hole
in my soul.
Never to be filled.
Yet, full of sorrow and acts distilled.

Deep. Empty. Hollow.
But, we shall wait
in the hope of being in a better state.

Regardless of what I do,
Who I am,
and what I accumulate for.
The hole just rumbles and collapses on itself

At peace or war.
There is a gaping hole
in my soul that's not accounted for.

It started raining when we kissed

It hurts to kiss you
you gave me all you have.
And I?
I left you
with nothing but myself.

Pulling me in your arms
You kissed me
And it rained
It was cliche

I will remember the way
you made our little space feel
The way you brought me
Sunshine in the morning and
Calmness like sea

The light from the window,
Your pile of books and DVDs
Your push for black coffee
And,
My existence awfully

Together, our bodies flowed, crying.
It was meant to be

Healing hearts that we didn't break
It rained when we kissed

It still hurts to kiss you
you gave me all you have.
And I?
I left you
with nothing but myself.

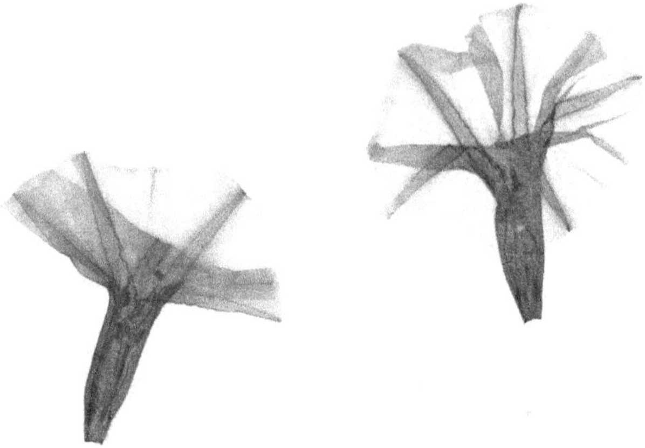

3:33

Precisely at this hour,
you discover, while
everyone around you is secure
you are often spiralling.

Your thoughts,
swirl as a result
of all the monsters.
Holding you from sinking
into the black ocean.

The heart tangled
as you continue to descend;
the moment your first tear falls,
it's as if you've summoned an end.

You are disoriented,
dissolving piece by piece,
lost, and drowning.
In your own sorrow,
lying still in the chaotic surrounding.

As opposed to
all the issues in your life,
You wish you had spent this night
counting stars.

Like walking on the edge of a knife
You lie there stiff, still, and behind bars.

www.ingramcontent.com/pod-product-compliance
Lightning Source LLC
Chambersburg PA
CBHW051734130826
49812CB00033B/850
9789357215770